Bond Book

This book is one of 155,000 in a special purchase to upgrade the CALS collection. Funds for the project were approved by Little Rock voters on 8/17/04.

Fish

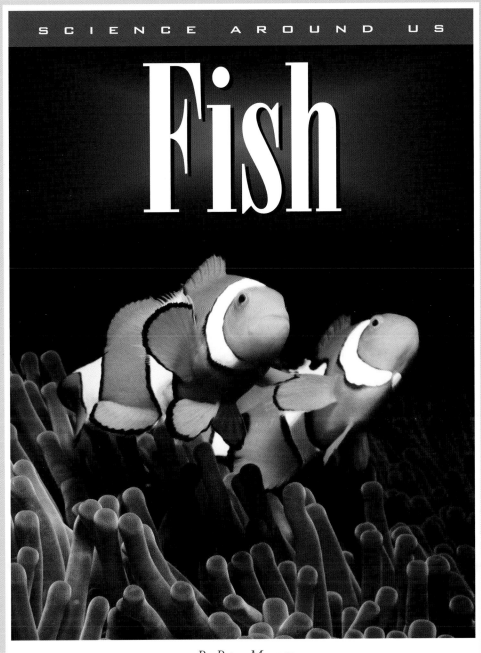

By Peter Murray

THE CHILD'S WORLD®
CHANHASSEN, MINNESOTA

The Child's World

Published in the United States of America by The Child's World®
PO Box 326, Chanhassen, MN 55317-0326
800-599-READ
www.childsworld.com

Content Advisers:
Jim Rising, PhD,
Professor of Zoology,
University of Toronto,
Department of Zoology,
Toronto, Ontario,
Canada, and Trudy
Rising, Educational
Consultant, Toronto,
Ontario, Canada

Photo Credits:
Cover/frontispiece: Jeffrey L. Rotman/Corbis; cover corner: Jeffrey L. Rotman/Corbis.
Interior: Animals Animals/Earth Scenes: 8 (Gerard Lacz), 15 (Carmela Leszczynski), 16
(OSF/D. Fleetham), 17 (Color-Pic), 19 (Mickey Gibson), 21 (Chris McLaughlin), 25
(OSF/David Thompson), 26 (James Watt); Corbis: 7 (Ivor Fulcher), 9 (Stephen Frink),
10 (Brandon D. Cole), 14 (Amos Nachoum), 20 (Hal Beral), 23 (Anthony Bannister),
27 (James A. Sugar); Digital Vision/Punchstock: 13. Marilyn Kazmers/Dembinsky Photo
Associates: 6; Patrick J. Lynch/Photo Researchers: 5; Jeffrey L. Rotman/Corbis: 12, 24.

The Child's World®: Mary Berendes, Publishing Director

Editorial Directions, Inc.: E. Russell Primm, Editorial Director; Pam Rosenberg, Line
Editor; Katie Marsico, Assistant Editor; Matt Messbarger, Editorial Assistant; Susan
Hindman, Copy Editor; Susan Ashley, Proofreader; Peter Garnham, Terry Johnson,
Olivia Nellums, Katherine Trickle, and Stephen Carl Wender, Fact Checkers; Tim
Griffin/IndexServ, Indexer; Cian Loughlin O'Day, Photo Researcher; Linda S. Koutris,
Photo Selector

The Design Lab: Kathleen Petelinsek, Design and Page Production

Library of Congress Cataloging-in-Publication Data
Murray, Peter, 1952 Sept. 29–
 Fish / by Peter Murray.
  v. cm. — (Science around us)
Includes bibliographical references (p.   ).
Contents: What makes a fish?—Skeletons, scales, fins, and teeth—Cold-blooded water-
breathers—Senses and defenses—Reproduction—Kinds of fish.
 ISBN 1-59296-214-9 (lib. bdg. : alk. paper) 1. Fishes—Juvenile literature. [1. Fishes.]
I. Title. II. Science around us (Child's World (Firm))
 QL617.2.M87 2004
 597—dc22   2003027218

TABLE OF CONTENTS

WHAT MAKES A
FISH A FISH?

Five hundred million years ago, there were no fish.

Squiggly creatures, ancestors to modern fishes, swam

through the seaweed, feeding on tiny one-celled life forms called

protozoa. Blobs of living jelly—jellyfish—floated on the surface of

the sea. Mollusks and crustaceans explored the ocean's sandy bottom.

Earth's waters were full of swimming, floating, and crawling crea-

tures—but none of them were fish as we know them today.

The first primitive fish appeared in the oceans about 450 mil-

lion years ago. They probably **evolved** from the ancestors of a

tiny creature called the lancelet.

Lancelets have gill slits, a stiff spine made of **cartilage,** and

a nerve cord running along the spine. They look like guppies, but

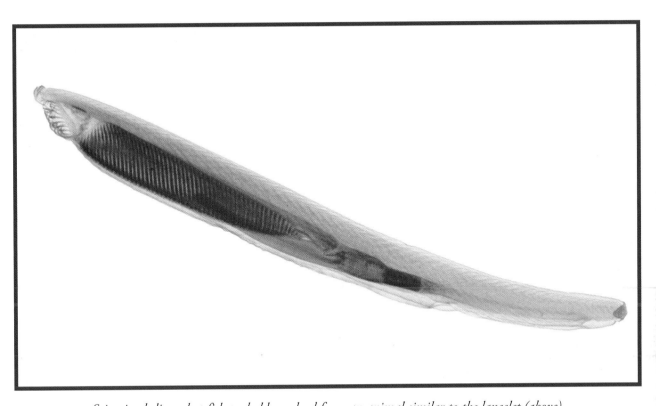

Scientists believe that fish probably evolved from an animal similar to the lancelet (above).

they have no eyes, scales, jaws, or teeth. Their flattened tails move them quickly through the water. You might think of the lancelet as an "almost fish."

Today, there are more **species** of fish than all the types of mammals, birds, reptiles, and amphibians combined. But what exactly makes a fish different from a salamander or a duck or a scuba diver?

*Many people learn more about fish by scuba diving
near places where fish are found, such as coral reefs.*

When you think of a fish, you probably imagine a **stream-lined,** water-breathing animal with a tail, fins, scales, and eyes. Most fish—from the tiny minnow to the ferocious great white shark—fit that description. But what about oddly shaped fish such as sea horses, eels, and rays? What exactly makes a fish a fish?

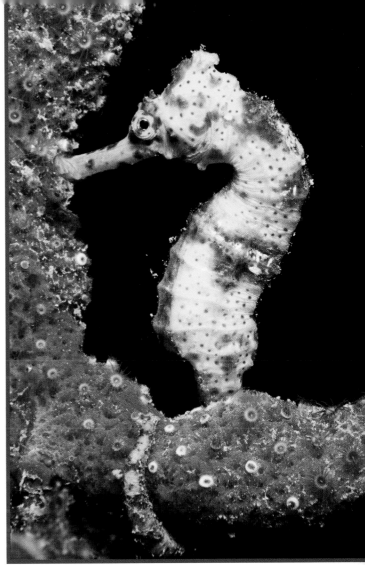

Sea horses don't look like most other fish. They usually live among seaweed and other plants and are not strong swimmers.

Are dolphins fish?
No. Dolphins and whales look like fish, but they are warm-blooded, air-breathing mammals.

CHAPTER TWO

SKELETONS, SCALES, FINS, AND TEETH

A fish is a water-dwelling **vertebrate** with fins, a tail, and gills. Fish were the first animals to have backbones and **internal** skeletons. Sea creatures such as clams, sea jellies, and shrimp do not have spines or internal skeletons. They are not fish.

At first glance, a fish skeleton looks very different from a human skeleton, but in many ways it is similar. Fish and people are both vertebrates—they have a spinal cord of nerve tissue protected by a flexible backbone. Fish have bony ribs to protect their inner organs and a hard

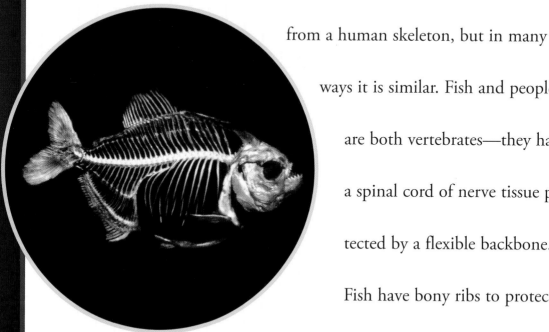

A piranha skeleton shows the flexible backbone, ribs, and skull that are common to all fish.

Tarpon have beautiful, shiny scales that are sometimes used to make jewelry.

Sharks and rays have skeletons made from cartilage. These flexible fish have roamed the oceans for about 400 million years.

skull to protect their brain. Most modern fish also have jaws with teeth and four "limbs," or movable fins.

Most fish are covered with a protective layer of hard plates called scales. Scales can be large or small, rough or smooth. Sharkskin is so abrasive it can be used as sandpaper. Tarpon have beautiful, flat scales more than 5 centimeters (2 inches) across. They are sometimes used to make jewelry. Eel scales are so tiny that they cannot be seen without a magnifying glass.

Flying fish sometimes use their large pectoral fins to "fly" through the air for short distances.

A typical fish has seven fins. The dorsal and anal fins are used to keep the fish from tipping. They work much like the tail of an airplane or the **keel** of a boat. The tail fin gives the fish power and speed—a sailfish can use its powerful tail to reach speeds up to 100 kilometers (60 miles) per hour. Most fish also have two pelvic fins for steering and two pectoral fins for turning and stopping.

The shape, size, and purpose of fins vary from fish to fish. Flying fish use their enormous pectoral fins to glide through the air for short distances. Rays use their huge pectoral fins to "fly" through the water and their long, whiplike tails for steering.

Most fish have teeth and jaws that move. **Predators** such as barracuda and piranhas have sharp teeth for holding and ripping apart **prey.** Plant eaters have teeth designed for cutting and grinding.

The scariest-looking teeth in the ocean belong to sharks. Shark teeth are constantly growing. When one tooth breaks or wears down, a new tooth moves forward to replace it. A shark can go through thousands of teeth in its lifetime.

Piranhas are much smaller than sharks, but their teeth are just as deadly. The piranha's jaw and sharp, triangular teeth are designed to rip chunks of flesh from larger animals. A hungry school of piranhas

The teeth of a parrot fish are joined together to form a hard beak which is used to break off and crush hard pieces of coral.

can kill and devour animals as large as deer—or even humans!

Parrot fish teeth are fused together into a hard beak capable of breaking off and crushing chunks of coral. The forceps fish has a long mouth that looks like a pair of tweezers. This fish finds its food deep in the cracks and crevices of coral.

COLD-BLOODED
WATER-BREATHERS

Fish live wherever there is water, from the warm coral reefs of

the Caribbean to the icy seas of the Arctic. But fish have no

fur or feathers, and they don't wear wool sweaters, so how do they

stay warm?

The warm waters near coral reefs are home to many fish.

Tuna are one of the few fish that are warm-blooded and can keep warm even in cold water.

They don't! Most fish are **ectotherms.** Their body temperature rises and falls with the temperature of the surrounding water. A few fast-swimming fish such as tuna, sailfish, and certain sharks are warm-blooded. Their ability to keep their muscles warm helps them swim quickly even in cold water.

We get our oxygen from the air by breathing air in and out of our lungs. Fish do not have lungs. Instead, they "breathe" by gulping water in through their mouths and pushing it out through their gills. The water passes through layers of spongy gill tissue, where tiny blood vessels absorb oxygen directly from the water.

A few fish have adapted to breathing air. The African lungfish lives in lakes that sometimes dry up during the summer. The lungfish buries itself in mud and breathes air until rainwater fills the lake again.

Sharks do not gulp water like other fish. Instead, they swim constantly, even when they are asleep. The motion of their bodies forces water into their mouths and out through their gills.

The lungfish is able to survive by burrowing in the mud of a dried up lake bed and breathing air until the lake fills with water again.

CHAPTER FOUR

SENSES AND DEFENSES

Like humans, fish can see, hear, smell, taste, and feel.

Fish that live in shallow, clear water—where there is a lot of light—see in color and have excellent eyesight. Species that live in dark or murky water rely on their keen sense of smell. Sharks can smell the slightest bit of blood in the water. Catfish living on the

Raccoon butterfly fish swim off the coast of the Hawaiian island of Maui.
Fish that live in shallow waters have good eyesight and can see colors, unlike
fish that live in deep waters where little sunlight can reach them.

bottoms of muddy rivers use their sensitive nostrils and feelers to find food.

Catfish live near the muddy bottoms of lakes and rivers. They rely on their feelers to help them find food.

Most people think that fish taste good as food—but do fish also have a sense of taste? Yes! Fish tongues are covered with taste buds. A fish constantly tastes the water that flows into its mouth. Migrating fish such as salmon use taste and smell to help guide them back to the rivers where they were born.

Although fish do not have **external** ears as we do, they do have a good sense of hearing. Sound waves carry quickly through water, and fish sense the vibrations with their bodies. The sound is carried through their skeletons to their inner ears.

Many fish also have a sense that we humans lack. Along each side of the fish, running from head to tail, is a row of cells called the lateral line. These cells are extremely sensitive, detecting any movement or change in water **pressure.** The lateral line is like a sixth sense.

Sharks, catfish, and some other fish have yet another sense—they produce an electrical field that surrounds them like a bubble. Any fish that touches this invisible field will be noticed.

It's a fish-eat-fish world down there. To avoid getting eaten, smaller fish have to be **agile** and alert. If you've ever tried to catch a small fish with your bare hands, you know how quick they can be.

Schooling is a way for fish to seek safety. When thousands of fish are swimming together, predators become confused and can't pick out an individual fish.

Blue snappers swim together, or school. This behavior helps keep them safe from predators.

Many fish have **camouflage** markings that make them hard to see. When a predator passes by, the fish remain still so they are less likely to be noticed.

Some species have developed unusual defenses. The dorsal fins of lionfish and stonefish have evolved into deadly, poisonous spines.

Lionfish have sharp, poisonous dorsal fins which help keep predators away.

Any animal that tries to eat a puffer fish will get a surprise when it suddenly puffs its body up to three times its normal size!

The puffer fish makes itself hard to swallow by suddenly inflating to three times its original size. The surgeonfish has a sharp bone near its tail that it can pop out like a switchblade—one flick of its tail can inflict serious damage on a predator.

CHAPTER FIVE

REPRODUCTION

Q: Why is a cod like a chicken?

A: They both lay eggs.

But chickens lay one egg a day. One cod can lay up to 30 million eggs at one time! Cod lay large numbers of eggs, but only one in a million will ever grow to be an adult fish.

Fish eggs must be **fertilized** by a male fish. In some species, the male and female fish school together. As the females release eggs, the males release sperm. The fertilized eggs float away. Those that are not eaten will hatch into tiny fish.

The male sunfish builds a nest on the sandy bottoms of lakes and ponds. The nest looks like a small crater. Female sunfish lay

their eggs in his nest. The male fertilizes the eggs and protects them

until they hatch.

Most sharks and a few other species

fertilize the egg while it is still inside

Some people like to eat fish eggs. Fish eggs are served as a rare treat called caviar. The finest caviar comes from the beluga sturgeon. One ounce can cost more than $100.

A tiny fish emerges from its egg. More fish will emerge from the other eggs nearby if they are not eaten by other sea creatures.

A baby tiger shark (above) develops inside its mother's body and is born looking like a smaller version of an adult shark.

the female. Female sharks do not release their eggs into the water. Baby sharks develop inside their mothers' bodies and are born as small sharks.

The survival rate of newborn fish is extremely low. Big fish eat little fish, and baby fish are gobbled up by the billions every minute of every day. Those newborns that reach adulthood will lay eggs of their own, and the cycle of life will continue.

CHAPTER SIX

KINDS OF FISH

Most of the fish in the world are classified as bony fish. This group includes minnows, trout, tuna, sturgeon, and swordfish—a total of about 25,000 species. Bony fish have a bony skeleton and movable jaws. Most bony fish also have a swim bladder—an internal air sac that keeps them from sinking to the bottom of the sea.

Minnows are one of the many kinds of fish called bony fish.
Bony fish make up the great majority of fish in the world.

A stingray is a cartilaginous fish—its skeleton is made of a soft, strong material known as cartilage.

Sharks, rays, and skates make up the cartilaginous fish. They are similar to the bony fish, but their skeletons are made of cartilage and they do not have a swim bladder. There are about 600 species of cartilaginous fish.

The snakelike lampreys and hagfish are the most primitive fish. They do not have jaws, and feed by attaching their round mouths to another fish—living or dead—and licking it with their rough tongues. These jawless fish have simple digestive systems, and they cannot swim very well.

Look for fish in bodies of water near you. Whether you are near a lake, a river, an ocean, or an aquarium, you can find opportunities to learn more about fish just about anywhere in the world.

Tide pools are great places to see fish and other sea creatures and learn more about them.

GLOSSARY

agile (AJ-il) Something that is agile can move quickly and with ease.

camouflage (KAM-uh-flaazh) Camouflage is coloring that makes an animal blend in with its surroundings.

cartilage (KAR-tuh-lij) Cartilage is the strong, rubbery material that makes up the skeletons of sharks, rays, and skates.

ectotherms (EK-tuh-thurmz) Ectotherms are animals whose body temperature rises and falls with the temperature of their environment, also called cold-blooded animals. Fish, reptiles, and amphibians are ectotherms.

evolved (ih-VOLVD) Something that has evolved has changed slowly over time.

external (ek-STUR-nul) Something that is external is on the outside.

fertilized (FUR-tuh-lized) When an egg is fertilized, a sperm has joined with it to begin the process of reproduction.

internal (in-TUR-nul) If something is internal, it is inside something else.

keel (KEEL) A keel is a long beam along the bottom of a boat.

predators (PRED-uh-turz) Predators are animals that hunt other animals for food.

pressure (PRESH-er) Pressure is the force produced by something pressing on something else.

prey (PRAY) An animal that is hunted by another animal for food is called prey.

species (SPEE-sheez) A species is a certain type of living thing. Fish of the same species can mate and produce young. Fish of different species cannot produce young together.

streamlined (STREEM-lined) Something that is streamlined can move quickly and easily through water or the air.

vertebrate (VUR-tuh-brayt) A vertebrate is an animal with a backbone and an internal skeleton. Mammals, birds, reptiles, amphibians, and fish are all vertebrates.

DID YOU KNOW?

- The porcupine fish has sharp, pointed scales. When threatened, it puffs up its body and its scales stick out like a porcupine's quills.

- Catfish have no scales. They rely on their thick skin and a heavy layer of slippery mucus for protection.

- A few million years ago, a giant shark named megalodon ruled the oceans. Megalodon had a mouth big enough to swallow a horse. Its sharp, serrated teeth were about 18 centimeters (7 inches) long.

- The sawfish has a long, bony snout lined with sharp teeth. It can whip its sawlike snout back and forth to kill its prey, or use it to dig in the sea bottom for buried crustaceans.

- With its pop-eyed stare and wide mouth, the mudskipper looks more like a frog than a fish. It uses its flippers to walk from pond to pond and is able to absorb oxygen directly from the air.

- Fish do not have eyelids. With water all around them, there is no danger of their eyeballs drying out.

- The markings on fish such as flounder and sole help them blend in with the ocean bottom.

- The stripes and spots on fish such as pipefish and sunfish make them almost invisible in their natural environment.

- The tiny sea horse might not look like a fish, but it has gills, fins, a bony skeleton, and jaws, so it is a bony fish.

- The whale shark is the largest fish in the ocean. The largest ever found is said to have been 18 meters (60 feet) long and weighed about 41,000 kilograms (90,000) pounds.

- Hagfish, which feed by burrowing into the bodies of dead fish, were once classified as worms. But a closer look showed that these strange-looking animals have both gills and fins. They are now classified as fish.

THE ANIMAL KINGDOM

VERTEBRATES

fish

amphibians

reptiles

birds

mammals

INVERTEBRATES

sponges

worms

insects

spiders & scorpions

mollusks & crustaceans

sea stars

sea jellies

HOW TO LEARN MORE ABOUT FISH

At the Library

Spilsbury, Richard, and Louise Spilsbury. *Classifying Fish.*
Chicago: Heinemann Library, 2003.

Stewart, Melissa. *Fishes.* New York: Children's Press, 2001.

Woods, Samuel G., and Jeff Cline (illustrator).
*The Amazing Book of Fish and Ocean Creature Records:
The Largest, the Smallest, the Fastest, and Many More!*
Woodbridge, Conn.: Blackbirch Marketing, 2000.

On the Web

VISIT OUR HOME PAGE FOR LOTS OF LINKS ABOUT FISH:
http://www.childsworld.com/links.html
Note to Parents, Teachers, and Librarians: We routinely verify our Web links to make
sure they're safe, active sites—so encourage your readers to check them out!

Places to Visit or Contact

JOHN G. SHEDD AQUARIUM
To see many different kinds of fish from all over the world
1200 South Lake Shore Drive
Chicago, IL 60605
312/939-2438

SMITHSONIAN NATIONAL MUSEUM OF NATURAL HISTORY
*To see the Ancient Seas exhibit and learn more
about the evolution of fish and other marine life*
10th Street and Constitution Avenue NW
Washington, DC 20560
202/357-2700

INDEX

About the Author

Peter Murray has written more than 80 children's books on science, nature, history, and other topics. An animal lover, Pete lives in Golden Valley, Minnesota, in a house with one woman, two poodles, several dozen spiders, thousands of microscopic dust mites, and an occasional mouse.